In the vast expanses
eternal blue sky, lies the spiritual legacy of a
powerful and ancient belief system that has
shaped the lives and culture of countless
generations: Tengrism. This indigenous
spirituality, deeply rooted in the reverence for
nature and the intricate balance of the cosmos, has
guided the hearts and minds of nomadic and semi-
nomadic peoples across the region for millennia.
Today, Tengrism is experiencing a renaissance, as
modern spiritual seekers look to reconnect with
the wisdom of their ancestors and the natural
world around them.

In "Tengrism: Embracing the Sky and Earth,"
we invite you to journey with us as we explore the
rich history, core tenets, and cultural significance
of this ancient spiritual tradition. Our exploration
will delve into the origins of Tengrism and its
development over time, as well as the beliefs and
practices that have sustained it through the ages.

At the heart of Tengrist philosophy lies the
concept of the interconnectedness of all living
things, which is beautifully encapsulated in the
reverence for Tengri, the eternal blue sky, and the

Earth, as well as the countless deities and spirits that comprise the Tengrist pantheon. Throughout this ebook, we will examine the sacred relationship between humanity, nature, and the divine, and how it is reflected in Tengrist rituals, ceremonies, and symbols.

Shamans, who serve as intermediaries between the human and spiritual realms, play a central role in Tengrist practice. As we delve into their world, we will gain insights into their training, initiation, and the ceremonies they perform to maintain harmony between the realms. Our exploration will also encompass the importance of sacred spaces and symbols, from the veneration of mountains and trees to the use of animal totems in rituals and art.

As we move through the chapters, we will discuss the influence of Tengrism on art, literature, and culture, both in its historical context and its modern-day expressions. We will also consider the role of Tengrism in shaping ecological thought and practice, exploring the spiritual insights it offers to help us build a more sustainable and harmonious future for our planet.

By the time we reach the end of our journey, we hope that you, too, will have come to appreciate the wisdom and beauty of Tengrism, and perhaps even feel inspired to integrate its teachings into your own life. Together, let us embrace the sky and earth as we uncover the secrets of this ancient spiritual tradition, and celebrate the enduring legacy of Tengrism in our rapidly changing world.

The History of Tengrism

Early Shamanic and Animistic Traditions

The spiritual roots of Tengrism can be traced back to the shamanic and animistic beliefs of the ancient tribes inhabiting the vast expanse of Siberia and Central Asia. These early belief systems were characterized by a deep connection to the natural world, with a central focus on the spirits and supernatural forces that were believed to inhabit the land, animals, plants, and even inanimate objects. In this context, shamans played a crucial role as mediators between the human and spiritual realms, utilizing their unique abilities to communicate with spirits, perform healing rituals, and offer guidance to their communities.

Emergence of Tengrist Elements

Over time, these early shamanic and animistic traditions began to incorporate new concepts and practices that would eventually coalesce into the spiritual framework of Tengrism. Among the most significant developments during this period was the emergence of Tengri, the eternal blue sky, as the supreme deity and embodiment of the divine force that governed the universe.

Tengri's association with the sky reflects the importance of celestial phenomena in the lives of ancient Central Asian peoples, who relied on the movements of the sun, moon, and stars for guidance in their nomadic travels and to mark the passage of time. This celestial orientation also laid the groundwork for the development of a complex pantheon of deities and spirits, each associated with specific natural elements or aspects of human existence.

Early Archaeological Evidence

The origins of Tengrism can be gleaned from various archaeological findings, such as petroglyphs, burial sites, and artifacts, which offer valuable insights into the spiritual beliefs and practices of ancient Central Asian tribes. Some of the earliest evidence of Tengrist elements can be found in the form of petroglyphs, which depict scenes of hunting, shamanic rituals, and celestial symbols, dating back to the Bronze Age (3000-2000 BCE).

Burial sites from this period also provide a wealth of information about early Tengrist practices, particularly in relation to the afterlife and ancestor veneration. The construction of kurgans, or burial mounds, and the inclusion of grave goods, such as weapons, ornaments, and even sacrificed animals, suggest a belief in an afterlife and the continued presence of ancestors in the spiritual realm.

Artifacts such as the Deer Stone statues, found in modern-day Mongolia and dating back to the late

Bronze Age, offer further evidence of Tengrist symbolism. These intricately carved megaliths feature images of flying deer, which are believed to represent the souls of the deceased, as well as other Tengrist motifs, such as the Tree of Life and celestial symbols.

Together, these archaeological discoveries paint a vivid picture of the early origins of Tengrism, offering a glimpse into the rich spiritual tapestry that would evolve over time into the complex belief system we know today.

The Role of Turkic and Mongolic Tribes

The expansion of Tengrism across the vast landscapes of Eurasia can be largely attributed to the migrations and conquests of various Turkic and Mongolic tribes. These tribes, united by a shared linguistic and cultural heritage, played a crucial role in disseminating Tengrist beliefs and practices throughout the region, from the steppes of Central Asia to the forests of Siberia, and even as far as Eastern Europe and China.

The mobility and adaptability of these nomadic and semi-nomadic tribes allowed them to forge alliances and establish trade networks with other cultures, further facilitating the spread of Tengrism. As Tengrist beliefs spread, they often became intertwined with local religious practices, resulting in a syncretic blend of spiritual traditions that allowed Tengrism to evolve and flourish in diverse cultural contexts.

Tengrism and the Turkic Khaganates

The early Turkic Khaganates, particularly the Göktürks (6th-8th centuries), were instrumental in the consolidation and dissemination of Tengrist beliefs. As the Göktürks established their vast empire, stretching from the Caspian Sea to the borders of China, they adopted Tengrism as their official state religion and sought to integrate Tengrist principles into their political and social institutions.

The Göktürk Khaganate, governed by a dual monarchy system, was believed to derive its legitimacy from the divine authority of Tengri, with the khagans (kings) serving as earthly representatives of the sky god. The adoption of Tengrism as a state religion helped to unite the diverse subjects of the Göktürk Empire and foster a shared spiritual identity that transcended linguistic and cultural boundaries.

The Mongol Empire and Tengrism

The Mongol Empire, founded by Genghis Khan in the early 13th century, would go on to become the largest contiguous land empire in history, stretching from Eastern Europe to the Pacific Ocean. Like the Turkic Khaganates before them, the Mongols embraced Tengrism as their state religion, further amplifying its influence and prestige.

Genghis Khan himself was a devout follower of Tengri, and he believed that his conquests were divinely sanctioned by the sky god. This belief in a divine mandate not only helped to legitimize Genghis Khan's rule but also served to galvanize his forces and create a sense of unity among his diverse subjects. The Mongol Empire's religious tolerance and syncretism allowed Tengrism to coexist alongside other faiths, such as Buddhism, Christianity, and Islam, contributing to its continued survival and adaptation in various cultural contexts.

The Legacy of Tengrism in Eurasia

Although Tengrism's influence waned with the decline of the Turkic and Mongol empires, its spiritual and cultural legacy continued to reverberate throughout the Eurasian landscape. Tengrist beliefs and practices became deeply ingrained in the folk traditions of many Central Asian and Siberian communities, persisting even in the face of the encroachment of other world religions.

Today, the resurgence of Tengrism as an alternative spiritual path is a testament to the enduring appeal and adaptability of this ancient belief system. Its continued relevance and influence across the vast expanse of Eurasia bear witness to the resilience and vitality of a spiritual tradition that has weathered the storms of history and emerged with renewed vigor in the modern world.

The Göktürk Khaganate and Tengrism

The Göktürk Khaganate, established in the 6th century CE, was a significant force in shaping the Tengrist spiritual landscape. As the first political entity to unite the diverse Turkic tribes under a single banner, the Göktürk Khaganate played a pivotal role in the development and dissemination of Tengrist beliefs and practices throughout the region.

The Göktürk rulers, who claimed to derive their authority from Tengri, the eternal blue sky, sought to integrate Tengrist principles into their political and social institutions. This integration was exemplified by the dual monarchy system, which was believed to be a reflection of the divine balance between the sky and earth. The adoption of Tengrism as the state religion not only helped to unify the diverse subjects of the Göktürk Empire but also fostered a shared spiritual identity that transcended linguistic and cultural boundaries.

The Uyghur Khaganate and Tengrism

Following the collapse of the Göktürk Khaganate, the Uyghur Khaganate emerged in the 8th century as the dominant power in Central Asia. The Uyghurs, like their Göktürk predecessors, embraced Tengrism as their official state religion, further consolidating its influence and prestige in the region.

Under Uyghur rule, Tengrism continued to evolve, absorbing elements of other religious traditions, such as Buddhism, Manichaeism, and Zoroastrianism. This syncretic approach allowed Tengrism to adapt to a variety of cultural contexts and facilitated the integration of diverse religious practices into its spiritual framework.

The Mongol Empire and the Role of Tengrism

The Mongol Empire, founded by Genghis Khan in the early 13th century, was instrumental in further spreading Tengrism across the Eurasian continent. As the largest contiguous land empire in history, the Mongol Empire brought Tengrism to the forefront of the spiritual landscape in the territories it conquered.

Genghis Khan, a devout follower of Tengri, believed that his conquests were divinely sanctioned by the sky god. This belief in a divine mandate not only helped to legitimize Genghis Khan's rule but also served to galvanize his forces and create a sense of unity among his diverse subjects.

The Mongol Empire was renowned for its religious tolerance and syncretism, which allowed Tengrism to coexist alongside other faiths, such as Buddhism, Christianity, and Islam. This inclusive approach contributed to the survival and adaptation of Tengrism in various cultural contexts, even as the influence of other world religions grew.

State Rituals and Ceremonies

Under the Turkic and Mongol empires, Tengrism was deeply ingrained in the fabric of daily life, shaping the rituals and ceremonies that marked important events and transitions. Among the most significant of these rituals were the enthronement ceremonies for new rulers, which typically involved invoking the blessings of Tengri and the ancestors to legitimize their reign.

The practice of offering animal sacrifices to Tengri and other deities was also common, symbolizing the connection between the human and spiritual realms and serving to maintain harmony and balance within the empire. These rituals, which often involved elaborate feasts and celebrations, played a crucial role in strengthening social cohesion and fostering a shared spiritual identity among the diverse subjects of the Turkic and Mongol empires.

Encounters with World Religions

As the influence of the Turkic and Mongol empires waned, Tengrism faced increasing competition from other world religions such as Buddhism, Islam, and Christianity. The spread of these faiths was often facilitated by political alliances, trade networks, and missionary activities, which contributed to the fragmentation and assimilation of Tengrist communities. The syncretic nature of Tengrism enabled it to incorporate elements of these other faiths into its spiritual framework, allowing for a gradual and often partial transition to new religious practices among Tengrist populations.

Tengrism under Islamic and Christian Domination

As Islam and Christianity gained prominence in Central Asia and the surrounding regions, Tengrist communities faced mounting pressure to convert to these faiths. In many cases, the adoption of Islam or Christianity was driven by political expediency, as rulers sought to forge alliances with powerful Islamic and Christian empires, or to strengthen their rule by adopting the religion of the majority of their subjects.

Despite these pressures, Tengrism persisted in pockets of Central Asia and Siberia as a folk religion, deeply embedded in the cultural fabric of these regions. In some cases, Tengrist beliefs and practices were integrated into local Islamic and Christian traditions, resulting in a unique fusion of spiritual beliefs that continued to evolve over time.

Soviet Era and the Suppression of Tengrism

During the Soviet era, Tengrism faced further challenges as state-sanctioned atheism became the norm in Central Asia and Siberia. Traditional religious practices, including Tengrism, were actively suppressed by the Soviet regime, which sought to eradicate religious belief in favor of a secular, communist ideology.

Despite these efforts, Tengrism managed to survive in the private sphere, passed down through generations within families and communities as an essential part of their cultural heritage. The resilience of Tengrism in the face of Soviet oppression can be attributed, in part, to its deep roots in the everyday lives and customs of its practitioners, as well as its adaptability in the face of external challenges.

The Modern Resurgence of Tengrism

In recent decades, Tengrism has experienced a remarkable resurgence in Central Asia and beyond, as people seek to reconnect with their ancestral roots and rediscover the spiritual wisdom of their forebears. This revival has been fueled, in part, by the collapse of the Soviet Union and the subsequent re-emergence of national identities and cultural pride among the newly independent states of the region.

The resurgence of Tengrism has also been driven by a growing global interest in indigenous spiritual traditions and alternative belief systems, which offer unique perspectives on the interconnectedness of all living things and our shared responsibility to protect and preserve the earth for future generations. Today, Tengrism is experiencing a renaissance as an alternative spiritual path, appealing to both its traditional practitioners and a new generation of spiritual seekers who are drawn to its timeless wisdom and deep reverence for the natural world.

Core Beliefs and Practices of Tengrism

Tengri, the Eternal Blue Sky, is the central deity and supreme creator in Tengrism, embodying the limitless expanse of the heavens and the eternal cycles of time. This section will explore the nature of Tengri, the deity's role as the source of life and order, and the significance of Tengri in relation to ancestral veneration in Tengrist practice.

The Nature of Tengri

Tengri is often described as an omnipotent, omnipresent, and incorporeal being, transcending the boundaries of time and space. As the embodiment of the sky, Tengri is associated with the color blue, symbolizing the infinite and all-encompassing nature of the heavens. Tengri is also considered to be a genderless deity, representing the unity and balance of the masculine and feminine aspects of the cosmos.

In Tengrist cosmology, Tengri is the highest power in the universe and the ultimate source of all creation. The deity's role as the supreme creator is reflected in Tengrist creation myths, which describe the genesis of the world as emanating from Tengri's divine will.

Tengri as the Source of Life and Order

As the supreme deity in Tengrism, Tengri is believed to be the source of life and the sustaining force that maintains the balance and harmony of the natural world. Tengri is said to have created the first humans and animals, imbuing them with the vital energy, or kut, needed to sustain life.

Tengri is also considered the guardian of cosmic order and the enforcer of moral laws, ensuring that balance is maintained between the realms of the sky, earth, and the underworld. This belief in Tengri's role as the ultimate arbiter of justice and harmony underscores the importance of ethical conduct and moral rectitude in Tengrist practice.

Tengri and the Ancestors

In Tengrism, the veneration of ancestors is a central aspect of spiritual practice, reflecting the belief in the interdependence of the living and the dead in maintaining the cosmic order. The ancestors are seen as intermediaries between the human and divine realms, serving as conduits for the flow of blessings and protection from Tengri to their descendants.

Tengrists believe that, upon death, the souls of their ancestors ascend to the sky, joining the ranks of Tengri's celestial retinue. In this capacity, the ancestors are believed to watch over their living kin, offering guidance and wisdom in times of need. The veneration of ancestors in Tengrist practice serves to maintain the spiritual connection between the living and the dead, ensuring the continued flow of kut, or life energy, from Tengri to the human world.

While Tengri occupies the highest position in the Tengrist pantheon, the spiritual universe of Tengrism is populated by a diverse array of lesser deities and spirits, each with their own unique attributes and functions. This section will delve into the nature and roles of these entities, as well as their relationships with humans in Tengrist practice.

Lesser Deities and Spirits

Beneath Tengri, the Tengrist pantheon encompasses a variety of deities, each presiding over specific aspects of the natural world or human life. Some of these deities include:

- Umay: A goddess of fertility, childbirth, and protection, Umay is believed to watch over women, children, and the family unit, ensuring their safety and well-being.
- Erlik: The god of the underworld, Erlik is responsible for the souls of the deceased and their journey to the afterlife. He is often portrayed as a trickster figure, testing the living and the dead alike.
- Koyash: The sun god, Koyash is a vital source of life and energy, illuminating the world and fostering growth and abundance.
- Ay Ata: The moon god, Ay Ata is associated with cold and night.

Nature Spirits and Sacred Animals

In addition to the deities, the Tengrist pantheon also features a multitude of nature spirits and sacred animals, which represent the diverse elements and forces of the natural world. These spirits are believed to inhabit various features of the landscape, such as rivers, mountains, and forests, and can be invoked for protection, guidance, or assistance.

Sacred animals play a significant role in Tengrist cosmology, embodying the qualities and attributes of the deities they represent. Some of the most prominent sacred animals in Tengrism include:

- The Wolf: A symbol of courage, loyalty, and strength, the wolf is often associated with the sky god Tengri and the legendary ancestors of the Turkic and Mongol peoples.
- The Horse: Revered for its power, grace, and endurance, the horse is a symbol of nobility and freedom in Tengrist tradition, and is closely linked to the sun god Koyash.
- The Bear: A symbol of wisdom, protection,

and healing, the bear is associated with the earth mother and the feminine aspects of the divine.

Interactions between Deities and Humans

In Tengrism, the relationships between humans and the deities and spirits of the pantheon are characterized by mutual respect, cooperation, and interdependence. Humans are seen as an integral part of the cosmic order, responsible for maintaining balance and harmony on earth through their actions and interactions with the spiritual realm.

Tengrists seek to cultivate and maintain positive relationships with the deities and spirits through prayer, offerings, and ritual. By honoring and appeasing these spiritual beings, Tengrists believe they can secure their blessings and protection, ensuring the continued flow of life energy and divine favor in their lives.

At the same time, Tengrists are expected to uphold the ethical principles and moral teachings of their faith, as a reflection of the divine order established by Tengri. In this way, the interactions between humans and the deities and spirits of the Tengrist pantheon serve to reinforce the importance of balance, harmony, and righteous conduct in the spiritual life of the Tengrist practitioner.

Shamans play a crucial role in Tengrist spirituality, acting as intermediaries between the human and spiritual realms. This section will examine the shamanic calling, the role of the shaman as a spiritual mediator, and the various rituals and practices associated with shamanism in Tengrism.

The Shamanic Calling

In Tengrism, the path of the shaman is often regarded as a divine calling, with prospective shamans receiving signs or visions that indicate their selection by the spirits. The shamanic calling is usually passed down through family lines, with the knowledge, skills, and spiritual connections being inherited from one generation to the next.

Once called to the shamanic path, initiates must undergo a rigorous period of training, which may involve periods of isolation, fasting, and meditation. This training is designed to cultivate the initiate's spiritual sensitivity and prepare them for the challenges and responsibilities of the shamanic vocation.

The Shaman as a Spiritual Mediator

As spiritual mediators, shamans bridge the gap between the human and spiritual realms, serving as channels for communication, healing, and guidance. Shamans are believed to possess the unique ability to enter a state of altered consciousness, known as a trance, which enables them to communicate directly with the spirits and deities of the Tengrist pantheon.

In their role as spiritual mediators, shamans perform various functions, including:

- Divination: Shamans are often called upon to seek guidance or insight from the spirits, using various methods such as dream interpretation, casting bones, or observing the behavior of animals.
- Healing: Shamans are believed to possess the power to diagnose and cure physical and spiritual ailments, often employing a combination of herbal remedies, energy healing, and ritual practices.
- Spirit negotiation: Shamans may act as intermediaries in disputes or conflicts involving spirits, working to restore harmony and balance between the human and spiritual realms.

Shamanic Rituals and Practices

Shamanic rituals and practices form an integral part of Tengrist spirituality, providing a means for the community to connect with the divine and maintain balance and harmony in their lives. Some of the key rituals and practices associated with Tengrist shamanism include:

- Drumming and chanting: Shamans often use drumming and chanting to enter a trance state, which allows them to communicate with the spirits and deities. The rhythmic beats of the drum and the repetitive nature of the chants help to induce an altered state of consciousness, facilitating the shaman's journey into the spiritual realm.
- Spirit journeys: During a spirit journey, the shaman's soul is believed to travel to the spiritual realm, where they can communicate directly with the deities and spirits. These journeys may be undertaken for various purposes, such as seeking guidance, healing, or knowledge.
- Offerings and sacrifices: Shamans often

perform rituals involving offerings or sacrifices to the spirits and deities, as a means of showing respect and gratitude, or seeking their favor and protection. Offerings may include food, drink, or other symbolic items, while animal sacrifices are performed in specific circumstances to honor and appease the deities.

Through their unique skills and spiritual connections, shamans play a vital role in Tengrist communities, helping to maintain the delicate balance between the human and spiritual realms, and ensuring the continued flow of divine blessings and protection.

Rituals and ceremonies play a central role in Tengrist spirituality, providing practitioners with a means to connect with the divine, express gratitude, and maintain balance and harmony in their lives. This section will discuss the various types of rituals and ceremonies commonly observed in Tengrist practice, including prayer and offerings to Tengri, life-cycle rituals, and seasonal celebrations and festivals.

Prayer and Offerings to Tengri

Prayer and offerings are fundamental aspects of Tengrist practice, allowing practitioners to communicate with Tengri and the other deities and spirits of the pantheon. Prayers are typically directed to Tengri, either individually or as part of a group, and may involve recitations, chants, or songs. The act of praying allows Tengrists to express their gratitude, request guidance or assistance, and reaffirm their commitment to the teachings and values of Tengrism.

Offerings are made to Tengri and other deities and spirits as a sign of respect, gratitude, and devotion. These offerings may include items such as food, drink, incense, or other symbolic gifts, which are presented during rituals or ceremonies. Offerings serve to acknowledge the benevolence of the divine and to secure their continued favor and protection.

Life-Cycle Rituals

In Tengrism, significant life events and milestones are marked by rituals and ceremonies that reaffirm the individual's connection to the divine and the community. Some examples of life-cycle rituals in Tengrist practice include:

- Birth: The birth of a child is celebrated with a ritual that involves prayers, offerings, and blessings to ensure the child's health, protection, and spiritual well-being.
- Coming of Age: Adolescents undergo a coming-of-age ceremony, marking their transition to adulthood and their assumption of the responsibilities and obligations that come with it.
- Marriage: Marriage ceremonies in Tengrist tradition are designed to unite not only the couple but also their families and ancestors, securing the blessings of the divine and the community for their union.
- Death: Funerary rituals in Tengrism seek to ensure the safe passage of the deceased to the afterlife, honor their memory, and maintain

the spiritual connection between the living and the dead.

Seasonal Celebrations and Festivals

Tengrists observe a variety of seasonal celebrations and festivals that honor the cycles of nature and the divine forces that govern them. These events serve to strengthen the bonds between the community, the natural world, and the spiritual realm, ensuring the continued flow of life energy and divine blessings. Some of the most significant Tengrist festivals include:

- Navruz (Spring Equinox): Celebrated around the 21st of March, Navruz marks the beginning of the new year and the renewal of life. The festival is characterized by feasting, dancing, and the performance of rituals to welcome the return of the sun and the blessings of Tengri.
- Tengri Ayt (Summer Solstice): Observed around the 21st of June, Tengri Ayt is a festival dedicated to the sky god Tengri, celebrating the sun at its zenith and the

abundance of the earth. The event involves rituals, games, and community gatherings, with participants expressing gratitude for the life-giving power of the sun.

- Tamga (Autumn Equinox): Celebrated around the 21st of September, Tamga marks the beginning of the harvest season and the transition from summer to winter. The festival is characterized by rituals of thanksgiving and offerings to the deities and spirits, acknowledging their role in ensuring a bountiful harvest.

Through the observance of rituals and ceremonies, Tengrist practitioners reaffirm their connection to the divine, the natural world, and their community. These practices serve to maintain balance and harmony in the lives of Tengrists, reinforcing the central teachings and values of their faith.

Rituals of Purification and Renewal

Purification and renewal are essential aspects of Tengrist spirituality, with rituals and ceremonies designed to cleanse the individual and the community of negative energies and restore balance and harmony. These practices may involve various elements, such as water, fire, or air, which are believed to possess purifying and transformative properties.

Some examples of purification and renewal rituals in Tengrist practice include:

- Ritual bathing: Water is considered a powerful purifying agent in Tengrist tradition, and ritual bathing serves to cleanse both the body and the spirit, washing away impurities and negative energies.
- Fire ceremonies: Fire symbolizes transformation and renewal in Tengrism, and fire ceremonies are often performed to purify the environment, burn away negativity, and invite the blessings of the deities and spirits.
- Smoke cleansing: Incense or smudge sticks

are often used in Tengrist rituals to cleanse and purify the atmosphere, with the fragrant smoke believed to carry prayers and intentions to the divine realm.

Through these rituals of purification and renewal, Tengrists seek to maintain a state of spiritual cleanliness and balance, ensuring that they remain in harmony with the divine and the natural world.

In summary, rituals and ceremonies form an integral part of Tengrist practice, providing a framework for practitioners to express their devotion, maintain balance and harmony in their lives, and strengthen their connections to the divine, the natural world, and their community. These practices serve to reinforce the core teachings and values of Tengrism, fostering a sense of unity and belonging among Tengrist practitioners.

Ethics and moral teachings are fundamental aspects of Tengrist spirituality, guiding the behavior and actions of practitioners in accordance with the principles of balance, harmony, and righteousness. This section will explore the key ethical principles of Tengrism, the concept of moral conduct, and the role of these teachings in fostering social cohesion and harmony.

Key Ethical Principles

The ethical principles of Tengrism are rooted in the belief in a cosmic order established by Tengri, which emphasizes balance, harmony, and interconnectedness. Some of the key ethical principles in Tengrist tradition include:

- Respect for nature: Tengrists believe that humans have a responsibility to protect and preserve the natural world, as all living beings are interconnected and dependent upon one another for survival.
- Honesty and integrity: Tengrists are encouraged to be truthful and transparent in

37

their interactions with others, upholding a strong sense of personal integrity and honor.

- Compassion and empathy: The teachings of Tengrism promote empathy and compassion for all living beings, encouraging practitioners to treat others with kindness and understanding.
- Generosity and hospitality: Tengrists are expected to be generous and hospitable, sharing their resources and providing assistance to those in need.
- Responsibility and accountability: Tengrists believe that each individual is responsible for their actions and the consequences of those actions, and should strive to be accountable for their behavior in both their personal and communal lives.

The Concept of Moral Conduct

In Tengrism, moral conduct is closely tied to the principles of balance and harmony, with practitioners encouraged to live in a manner that promotes the well-being of both the individual and the community. Tengrists believe that by adhering to the ethical teachings of their faith, they can maintain a state of harmony with the divine, the natural world, and their fellow human beings.

Moral conduct in Tengrism encompasses a range of behaviors, including:

- Observing rituals and ceremonies: Participating in the rituals and ceremonies of Tengrism helps to reinforce the spiritual and ethical values of the faith, fostering a sense of unity and belonging among practitioners.
- Practicing self-discipline: Tengrists are encouraged to cultivate self-discipline and restraint in their actions, thoughts, and speech, as a means of maintaining balance and harmony within themselves and their environment.

- Engaging in acts of charity and service: Tengrists believe that acts of charity and service are essential to the maintenance of social harmony, as they help to alleviate suffering and promote the welfare of the community.
- Respecting the rights and dignity of others: Tengrists are taught to respect the rights and dignity of all living beings, recognizing the inherent value and worth of each individual.

Ethics and Social Cohesion

The ethical teachings of Tengrism play a crucial role in fostering social cohesion and harmony among practitioners, promoting a sense of shared values and mutual respect. By adhering to the principles of balance, harmony, and righteousness, Tengrists are able to maintain a strong sense of communal identity and belonging, ensuring the continued stability and well-being of their communities.

In summary, the ethics and moral teachings of Tengrism provide a framework for practitioners to live in accordance with the principles of balance, harmony, and interconnectedness, fostering a sense of unity and belonging among Tengrist communities. These teachings serve to guide the behavior and actions of Tengrists, ensuring that they remain in harmony with the divine, the natural world, and their fellow human beings.

Tengrism has had a significant impact on the art, literature, and culture of the societies and communities where it is practiced. The rich symbolism, mythology, and spiritual beliefs of Tengrism have served as a source of inspiration and artistic expression throughout the centuries. This section will explore the influence of Tengrism on various aspects of art, literature, and culture, including visual arts, music, storytelling, and traditional crafts.

Visual Arts

Tengrist beliefs and symbolism have greatly influenced the visual arts in various forms, including painting, sculpture, and textiles. Common themes and motifs in Tengrist art include depictions of deities, spirits, and shamanic figures, as well as representations of the natural world, celestial bodies, and cosmic forces. These artistic expressions often serve to reinforce the spiritual and cultural values of Tengrism, reflecting the interplay of divine, human, and natural elements.

Music and Dance

Music and dance play a central role in Tengrist rituals, ceremonies, and celebrations, serving as a means of connecting with the divine, expressing devotion, and fostering a sense of communal identity. Tengrist music often incorporates the use of traditional instruments, such as drums, flutes, and stringed instruments, as well as vocal techniques, like throat singing and chanting.

Dance, too, is an integral aspect of Tengrist culture, with various forms and styles reflecting the unique beliefs, customs, and regional variations of Tengrist communities.

Storytelling and Literature

The rich mythology, folklore, and spiritual teachings of Tengrism have given rise to a wealth of storytelling and literary traditions. Epic tales, legends, and myths serve to convey the history, beliefs, and values of Tengrist communities, often featuring heroic figures, gods, spirits, and supernatural beings. Oral storytelling is a particularly important aspect of Tengrist culture, with stories passed down from generation to generation, preserving the knowledge and wisdom of the past.

Traditional Crafts

Tengrism has also had a significant influence on the traditional crafts and material culture of the communities where it is practiced. Skilled artisans create a wide range of objects imbued with Tengrist symbolism and meaning, such as carved wooden items, metalwork, ceramics, and textiles. These crafts often incorporate motifs and designs inspired by the natural world, celestial bodies, and Tengrist deities and spirits, reflecting the interconnectedness of the divine, human, and natural realms.

In summary, Tengrism has had a profound impact on the art, literature, and culture of the societies and communities where it is practiced. The rich symbolism, mythology, and spiritual beliefs of Tengrism have inspired a wide range of artistic expressions and cultural traditions, serving to reinforce the spiritual and cultural values of the faith and foster a sense of unity and belonging among Tengrist practitioners.

Modern Tengrism and its Revival

Historical Context

The resurgence of interest in Tengrism can be traced back to the late 20th and early 21st centuries, following the collapse of the Soviet Union and the subsequent political and cultural shifts in Central Asia. During the Soviet era, religious practices were heavily suppressed, and the promotion of atheism, combined with the policies of forced secularization and Russification, led to the erosion of traditional beliefs and customs in the region. With the collapse of the Soviet Union and the emergence of newly independent nations, there was a renewed interest in exploring and reclaiming indigenous spiritual traditions, including Tengrism.

Drivers of the Revival

The revival of Tengrism has been driven by various factors, including:

- Reassertion of national and ethnic identity: As the newly independent nations of Central Asia sought to assert their national identities and distinguish themselves from their Soviet past, many turned to their pre-Islamic and pre-Christian traditions, including Tengrism, as a source of inspiration and pride. This process of rediscovering and reclaiming ancestral traditions has played a significant role in the resurgence of Tengrist beliefs and practices.

- Spiritual exploration: In the post-Soviet era, there has been a growing interest in exploring diverse spiritual paths and alternatives to the dominant religions. Tengrism, with its deep historical roots and unique worldview, has attracted attention as a spiritual alternative that offers a distinct set of beliefs and practices, grounded in the cultural heritage of Central Asia.

- Ecological consciousness: The global rise of ecological awareness and the increasing concern for the environment have resonated with the core principles of Tengrism, which emphasize the interconnectedness of all living beings and the importance of living in harmony with the natural world. As a result, many individuals and communities have been drawn to Tengrism as a spiritual framework that supports and promotes ecological sustainability and stewardship.

Revival Movements and Initiatives

The revival of Tengrism has been supported and facilitated by a range of movements and initiatives, both at the grassroots and institutional levels. These include:

- The establishment of Tengrist organizations, associations, and study groups dedicated to the research, preservation, and promotion of

Tengrist traditions and knowledge. These organizations often collaborate with scholars, researchers, and practitioners to document and disseminate information on Tengrism, as well as to organize events, conferences, and workshops aimed at raising awareness and fostering dialogue on Tengrist beliefs and practices.

- The restoration and revitalization of Tengrist sacred sites, such as temples, shrines, and natural landmarks, which serve as important centers for the practice of Tengrist rituals and ceremonies, as well as repositories of cultural and spiritual heritage.

- The incorporation of Tengrist elements into educational curricula and cultural programs, as part of broader efforts to promote the appreciation and understanding of indigenous spiritual traditions and their contributions to national and regional identity.

Traditional Rituals and Ceremonies

The modern revival of Tengrism has led to the re-establishment of traditional rituals and ceremonies, both in private and public settings. Individuals and communities are increasingly participating in rituals such as offerings to Tengri, ancestral spirits, and other deities, as well as rites of passage, including weddings, funerals, and initiations. These ceremonies serve to strengthen the spiritual connection between practitioners and the divine, as well as to foster a sense of communal identity and belonging.

Tengrist Themes in Popular Culture

Tengrist themes and symbolism have made their way into popular culture, reflecting the growing interest in Tengrist beliefs and aesthetics. Examples include the incorporation of Tengrist imagery and motifs in visual arts, such as paintings, sculptures, and textiles, as well as the use of Tengrist narratives and themes in literature, music, and film. These contemporary expressions of Tengrism not only serve as a source of inspiration and artistic expression but also help to raise awareness of Tengrist beliefs and values among broader audiences.

Tengrist Organizations and Cultural Centers

The establishment of Tengrist organizations, associations, and cultural centers has played a crucial role in promoting the study, practice, and preservation of Tengrist traditions. These institutions often collaborate with scholars, researchers, and practitioners to document and disseminate information on Tengrism, as well as to organize events, conferences, and workshops aimed at raising awareness and fostering dialogue on Tengrist beliefs and practices. Cultural centers and museums dedicated to Tengrism also provide spaces for learning, reflection, and engagement with Tengrist art, artifacts, and historical documents.

Integration of Tengrist Principles in Environmental and Social Movements

Tengrist principles and values have been integrated into contemporary environmental and social movements, resonating with the global push for ecological sustainability, community resilience, and interfaith dialogue. For example, Tengrist-inspired environmental initiatives focus on the protection and restoration of natural habitats, the promotion of sustainable resource management, and the development of eco-spiritual practices that foster a deeper connection with the natural world. Social movements informed by Tengrism advocate for interfaith cooperation, the recognition of indigenous spiritual traditions, and the promotion of cultural diversity and inclusivity.

Tengrism in the Digital Age

With the advent of digital technology and social media, Tengrism has found new avenues for dissemination, networking, and engagement. Online platforms, such as blogs, forums, and social media groups, have facilitated the sharing of

Tengrist knowledge, resources, and experiences, connecting practitioners, scholars, and enthusiasts across geographical boundaries. Digital technology has also enabled the creation of virtual spaces for Tengrist rituals, ceremonies, and gatherings, as well as the development of educational materials, such as e-books, podcasts, and videos, that promote the understanding and appreciation of Tengrist beliefs and practices.

Contemporary manifestations of Tengrism encompass a wide range of expressions and initiatives that aim to promote the study, practice, and preservation of Tengrist traditions in the modern world. From the re-establishment of traditional rituals and ceremonies to the integration of Tengrist themes in popular culture and environmental movements, Tengrism continues to evolve and adapt to the challenges and opportunities of the 21st century, offering valuable insights and inspiration for those seeking to live in harmony with the divine, the natural world, and their fellow human beings.

As the modern revival of Tengrism continues to gain momentum, it faces a range of challenges and opportunities in navigating the complexities of the 21st-century world. Some of the key issues facing contemporary Tengrism include:

Balancing Tradition and Modernity

One of the primary challenges facing contemporary Tengrism is the need to balance the preservation of traditional beliefs and practices with the realities of modern life. Globalization, urbanization, and technological change have all had profound impacts on the ways in which people live, work, and interact with one another, posing both threats and opportunities for Tengrist communities. Tengrism must find ways to adapt and evolve while maintaining the integrity and authenticity of its core beliefs and values, ensuring that its teachings remain relevant and accessible to modern practitioners.

Engaging with Diverse Contexts

Another challenge facing contemporary Tengrism is the need to engage with diverse religious, cultural, and political contexts as it seeks to establish a place for itself within the contemporary spiritual landscape. Tengrism must navigate issues such as religious pluralism, interfaith dialogue, and political sensitivities, as well as address potential misconceptions and stereotypes about its beliefs and practices. Building bridges with other religious and cultural traditions, as well as fostering open and respectful dialogue, will be crucial to the ongoing success and growth of Tengrism in the modern world.

Addressing Misappropriation and Commercialization

As Tengrism gains popularity and visibility, there is a risk of misappropriation and commercialization of its beliefs, symbols, and practices. This can lead to the dilution of Tengrist teachings and the commodification of Tengrist culture, undermining the spiritual integrity and authenticity of the tradition. Tengrist communities must work to protect and preserve their cultural and spiritual heritage, while also finding ways to share their knowledge and wisdom in a responsible and respectful manner.

Promoting Ecological Sustainability and Social Justice

Tengrism has the opportunity to contribute meaningfully to global conversations on ecology, sustainability, and social justice, drawing on its unique perspectives and values. By promoting the interconnectedness of all living beings and the importance of living in harmony with the natural world, Tengrism can inspire and inform environmental initiatives, community resilience projects, and interfaith cooperation efforts. However, it must also contend with the realities of environmental degradation, social inequality, and political conflict, which can present significant obstacles to the realization of its ideals.

Fostering the Next Generation of Tengrist Practitioners

Finally, contemporary Tengrism faces the challenge of fostering the next generation of practitioners, ensuring that its teachings, traditions, and values are passed down to future generations. This will require the development of educational resources, mentorship programs, and community-building initiatives that engage and inspire young people, helping them to connect with their Tengrist heritage and cultivate a deep and lasting commitment to the path.

Conclusion

Throughout this book, we have explored the many facets of Tengrism, from its origins and history to its beliefs and practices. We have seen how Tengrism emphasizes the importance of harmony with nature, respect for the environment, and the interconnectedness of all things. We have also delved into the various rituals, ceremonies, and customs that are an integral part of Tengriism, and how they reflect the religion's core values and principles.

Moreover, we have examined the challenges that Tengrism has faced throughout its history, including persecution and suppression by more dominant religions and political systems. Despite these obstacles, Tengrism has managed to survive and evolve, adapting to new circumstances and continuing to provide spiritual guidance to its followers.

In conclusion, Tengrism is a fascinating and important religion that deserves to be better known and understood. Its emphasis on nature, harmony, and interconnectedness offers valuable insights into our relationship with the world around us, and its endurance over the centuries is a testament to the resilience and strength of the human spirit. By studying Tengrism and learning from its teachings, we can gain a deeper appreciation for the diversity and richness of human spirituality, and work towards building a more harmonious and sustainable world for all.

Printed in Great Britain
by Amazon